# U.S. Regions

# The Natural Environment of the Northeast

Blaine Wiseman

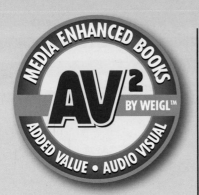

AV² provides enriched content that supplements and complements this book. Weigl's AV² books strive to create inspired learning and engage young minds in a total learning experience.

## Your AV² Media Enhanced books come alive with...

**Audio**
Listen to sections of the book read aloud.

**Key Words**
Study vocabulary, and complete a matching word activity.

**Video**
Watch informative video clips.

**Quizzes**
Test your knowledge.

Go to **www.av2books.com**, and enter this book's unique code.

## BOOK CODE

**F622990**

**Embedded Weblinks**
Gain additional information for research.

**Slide Show**
View images and captions, and prepare a presentation.

**AV² by Weigl** brings you media enhanced books that support active learning.

**Try This!**
Complete activities and hands-on experiments.

**... and much, much more!**

Published by AV² by Weigl
350 5th Avenue, 59th Floor
New York, NY 10118

Websites: www.av2books.com     www.weigl.com

Library of Congress Control Number: 2014942111

ISBN 978-1-4896-1230-4 (hardcover)
ISBN 978-1-4896-1231-1 (softcover)
ISBN 978-1-4896-1232-8 (single-user eBook)
ISBN 978-1-4896-1233-5 (multi-user eBook)

Printed in the United States of America in North Mankato, Minnesota
1 2 3 4 5 6 7 8 9  18 17 16 15 14

062014
WEP060614

Project Coordinator: Aaron Carr
Design: Mandy Christiansen

Every reasonable effort has been made to trace ownership and to obtain permission to reprint copyright material. The publishers would be pleased to have any errors or omissions brought to their attention so that they may be corrected in subsequent printings.

Weigl acknowledges Getty Images as its primary image supplier for this title.

# Contents

# U.S. Regions

The United States covers 3,794,083 square miles (9,826,630 square kilometers) of area. The 50 states are grouped into five major regions. They are the Northeast, the Southeast, the Midwest, the Southwest, and the West. Each region has different types of land, plants, animals, and **climates**.

**Legend**

- ■ West (11 states)
- ☐ Southwest (5 states)
- ☐ Northeast (11 states)
- ■ Southeast (11 states)
- ▨ Midwest (12 states)

**The Northeast borders the Southeast, the Midwest, Canada, and the Atlantic Ocean.**

**The Northeast covers 196,220 square miles (508,208 sq. km).**

Washington

Oregon

Montana

Idaho

Nevada

Wyoming

Utah

California

Colorado

Arizona

New Mexico

*Pacific Ocean*

MEXICO

Alaska

0 — 500 Miles
0 — 500 Kilometers

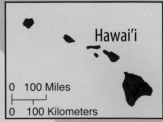
Hawai'i

0 100 Miles
0 100 Kilometers

CANADA

North
Dakota

Minnesota

*Lake
Superior*

New
Hampshire

Maine

Vermont

South
Dakota

Wisconsin

*Lake
Huron*

*Lake Ontario*

Massachusetts

New York

Rhode
Island
Connecticut

Nebraska

Iowa

*Lake
Michigan*

Michigan

*Lake Erie*

Pennsylvania

New
Jersey

UNITED STATES

Illinois

Indiana

Ohio

Delaware
Maryland

West
Virginia

Virginia

Kansas

Missouri

Kentucky

North Carolina

Oklahoma

Tennessee

South
Carolina

Arkansas

Alabama

Georgia

*Atlantic
Ocean*

N

Texas

Mississippi

Louisiana

Florida

*Gulf of Mexico*

0        250 Miles

0      250 Kilometers

# What Makes the Northeast?

Compared to the other four U.S. regions, the Northeast covers the smallest amount of land. However, it is a densely populated area of the country. The natural features of the Northeast have had a big impact on the development, history, and culture of the United States. This region includes rugged mountains, vast forests, wandering rivers, two Great Lakes, islands of all sizes, and scenic coastline.

Harbor seals live in the coastal waters of the Northeast as far south as New Jersey.

The northeastern tip of the country features the Atlantic Ocean coastline and the Appalachian Mountains. From Maine, the forested peaks of the Appalachians run through almost every state in the Northeast and extend as far south as Alabama. The Appalachians include New Hampshire's White Mountains and Vermont's Green Mountains. The largest state in the Northeast is New York. This state reaches from the Great Lakes in the west to Long Island on the coast. On the west side of the Appalachians, the mountains flatten to a **plateau** in Pennsylvania. From Massachusetts south to Maryland, cities and towns dominate the landscape. The East Coast provides important **natural resources** to the people, plants, and animals of every state in the Northeast, and beyond.

# Major Landmarks of the Northeast

The Northeast has many natural landmarks. The Appalachians are some of the world's oldest mountains. Cape Cod in eastern Massachusetts, formed by **glaciers**, extends in a long arc into the Atlantic Ocean. The Niagara River flows from Lake Erie into Lake Ontario, passing through a set of three waterfalls. The biggest of these is Horseshoe Falls in Canada. It is also called Canadian Falls. The other two, American Falls and Bridal Veil Falls, are in New York State. The three waterfalls combine to create Niagara Falls, one of the most powerful waterfalls on Earth.

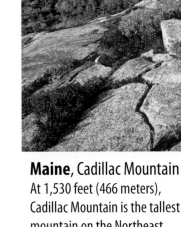

**Maine**, Cadillac Mountain
At 1,530 feet (466 meters), Cadillac Mountain is the tallest mountain on the Northeast coast. It is located on Mount Desert Island in Maine's Acadia National Park.

🍃 The height of American Falls ranges between 70 and 110 feet (21 and 34 m). This measurement is from the top of the falls to the top of the rock pile at the bottom.

**Massachusetts**,
Great Marsh
The Great Marsh is
20,000 acres (8,000 hectares)
of coastal **wetlands**. It is
also called a salt marsh. The
Great Marsh supports many
animal **species**.

**New Jersey and Pennsylvania**,
Delaware Water Gap
A 1,000-foot (300-m) valley cuts through
the Appalachians on the border of New
Jersey and Pennsylvania. The Delaware
Water Gap has been carved by the
Delaware River over millions of years.

**New York**, Watkins Glen
In the Finger Lakes region of New
York, a stream has carved 200-foot
(60-m) cliffs into the ground at
Watkins Glen. As the water flows
downstream, it creates 19 waterfalls,
as well as a series of pools that are
popular with swimmers.

# New York,
## Niagara Falls

**Niagara Falls was
created about
10,000
years ago.**

About
**20 million**
people visit
Niagara Falls
every year.

**The water
flowing over
Niagara Falls could
fill 68 Olympic-size swimming
pools in one minute.**

# Major Biomes of the Northeast

Large communities of living things, defined by their climate and plant life, are called biomes. Deserts, grasslands, and **tundra** are examples of biomes. The Northeast has other kinds of biomes. **Deciduous** forests cover most of this region. Farthest north, the types of trees change. Trees that have wide leaves give way to trees with pine needles that stay green year-round. Areas with many trees that bear cones, such as evergreens, are called coniferous forests.

## Mapping the Biomes of the Northeast

Use the map below and the information on the next page to answer the following questions.

1. How many states have more than one biome?
2. How many states have a deciduous forest biome?
3. What types of plants grow in a deciduous forest biome?

Maine

Vermont

New Hampshire

Lake Ontario

New York

Massachusetts

Lake Erie

Rhode Island

Connecticut

Pennsylvania

New Jersey

Maryland

Delaware

N

0        500 Miles

0        500 Kilometers

## Deciduous Forest

Climate: Seasonal

Vegetation: Dense leafy trees, flowers

Temperature: -22° to 86° Fahrenheit

(-30° to 30° Celsius)

## Coniferous Forest

Climate: Seasonal

Vegetation: Evergreen trees

Temperature: -4° to 104° F

(-20° to 40° C)

The common, or Atlantic, puffin can catch and carry many small fish in its beak. The diving bird is part of coastal ecosystems in the Northeast.

# Ecosystems of the Northeast

**P**lants and animals live together in smaller areas within a biome. These living things and their environment create an ecosystem. There are many different types and sizes of ecosystems. New York City could be considered a large ecosystem in the Northeast. Even where there are millions of people, coyotes, raccoons, rats, birds, fish, and insects can live. Humans are a part of the New York City ecosystem, too. A smaller ecosystem can exist within a larger one. Central Park in New York City is an example of a smaller ecosystem inside a larger one.

## Food for Thought

The food cycle connects each member of an ecosystem. Every plant and animal takes part in the food cycle. Plants make their food from energy in sunlight and from water and **nutrients** in the soil. After the Sun shines and rain falls, plants grow strong. Plant-eating animals, called herbivores, and **omnivores** feed on these plants. Then, **carnivores** eat the plant-eaters, taking nutrients from the meat. When animals die, they decompose, or break down. This process returns nutrients to the soil for plants to use, and the cycle starts again.

## Food Cycle

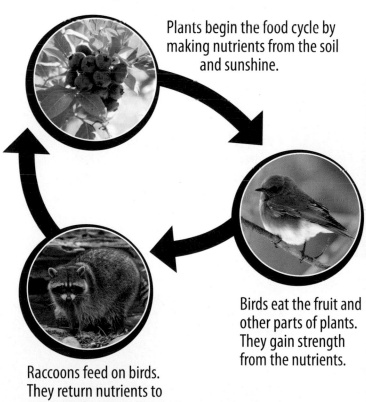

Plants begin the food cycle by making nutrients from the soil and sunshine.

Birds eat the fruit and other parts of plants. They gain strength from the nutrients.

Raccoons feed on birds. They return nutrients to the soil when they die.

## Eco Facts

New England lobsters use one claw to crush and the other to pinch and tear food.

More than **40** types of snakes live in the Chesapeake Bay area.

There are **FIVE** Atlantic puffin colonies, or groups, along the Maine coast.

**Karner blue butterflies eat wild blue lupine. In the Northeast, they live only where this plant grows in New York and New Hampshire.**

*Blue whales near the Atlantic coast eat up to*

**4 TONS** *(3.6 tonnes) of tiny animals called krill every day.*

# Major Rivers of the Northeast

**R**ivers in the Northeast are not the longest, largest, or most powerful in the United States. However, they have carved the land, connected different areas, and formed barriers that shape the region. For thousands of years, people have used these rivers to travel and move goods, building communities along their banks. Through warm summers and frozen winters, these rivers are also home to animal and plant communities all over the region.

**Pennsylvania**, Susquehanna River
This river winds almost 450 miles (725 km) through New York, Pennsylvania, and Maryland. The Susquehanna empties into Chesapeake Bay.

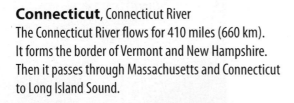

**Connecticut**, Connecticut River
The Connecticut River flows for 410 miles (660 km). It forms the border of Vermont and New Hampshire. Then it passes through Massachusetts and Connecticut to Long Island Sound.

**New Jersey**, Delaware River
The 405-mile (650-km) Delaware River supplies 15 million people with drinking water. It serves as part of the New York, Pennsylvania, New Jersey, and Delaware state borders.

**Maryland**, Potomac River
Two branches of the Potomac River begin in the mountains of West Virginia and come together in Maryland. The river flows through Washington, D.C. After 383 miles (616 km), it ends in Chesapeake Bay.

**New York**, Hudson River
The Hudson River forms in the Adirondack Mountains. It flows south for 315 miles (507 km) through eastern New York. The waterway is named after the sea captain Henry Hudson, who explored it in 1609.

# River Facts

The Susquehanna is almost **1 mile** (1.6 km) wide at Harrisburg, Pennsylvania.

The Connecticut River begins at a beaver pond near the Canadian border.

The southern part of the Hudson River is an estuary. That means it is a water passage where saltwater from the ocean meets a river.

The **SIX** New England states are Connecticut, Maine, Massachusetts, New Hampshire, Rhode Island, and Vermont. The region's longest river is the Connecticut River.

# Mammals of the Northeast

**W**ith so many humans living near and in the natural areas of the Northeast, it can be difficult for **mammals** to survive there. Pollution is another major threat to natural **habitats** such as the ocean. **Endangered** mammals in the Northeast include the right whale and the sperm whale.

**Massachusetts,** Right Whale
Only a few hundred right whales exist in the world. These huge animals are about 50 feet (15 m) long. That is about the length of a school bus.

**New Jersey,** Horse
Many U.S. states have official horses. New Jersey is the only state that has chosen all species of horse as its symbol.

**Connecticut,** Sperm Whale
Sperm whales are able to dive as deep as 2 miles (3 km). They can stay below the surface for more than an hour.

## Vermont, Morgan Horse

The first Morgan horse was born in 1789. It lived until it was 32. The horse is named after a music teacher and horse breeder named Justin Morgan.

## New Hampshire and Pennsylvania, White-tailed Deer

The white-tailed deer is the most common large mammal in North America.

## New York, Beaver

Beavers are known as nature's engineers because they build their **dams** so well. By constructing a dam in a stream, a beaver can create a new ecosystem. The pond that forms near a beaver dam gives the animal all the food it needs.

## Delaware, Gray Fox

The gray fox is the only member of the dog family that is able to climb trees. Active at night, these foxes jump from branch to branch as they hunt.

## Maine, Moose

A moose's antlers can be as wide as 6 feet (1.8 m).

## Maryland, Chesapeake Bay Retriever

Maryland's state dog is used for hunting. It sometimes even breaks through ice to retrieve items from the water in the winter. These dogs were bred over many years in the Chesapeake Bay area.

# Reptiles and Amphibians of the Northeast

**B**oth reptiles and amphibians are **cold-blooded** animals. However, there are important differences between them. Amphibians have smooth skin. They are born from eggs in or near the water and begin life there, breathing through gills like fish. Later, they change into adults, growing lungs and moving to the land. Reptiles have skin covered in dry **scales**. They lay their eggs or give birth on land. Mammals, birds, and fish often hunt reptiles and amphibians. Where reptiles and amphibians are plentiful, other animals are well fed. Protecting wetland and forest habitats helps reptiles, amphibians, and their ecosystems to survive.

About **3,500** frog and toad species exist in the world.

There are about **360 species** of newts and salamanders.

## Official State Amphibians

**New Hampshire,**
Spotted Newt

The spotted newt is one of the few salamander species **native** to North America. It was the first official state amphibian in the United States. The newt feeds mostly on mosquito **larvae**.

**Vermont,**
Northern Leopard Frog

Northern leopard frogs can be as long as 5 inches (12.7 centimeters). Females tend to be slightly larger than males. These frogs sometimes live in fields. That is why they are also called meadow frogs.

# Official State Reptiles

**Maryland,** Diamondback Terrapin Turtle

Diamondback terrapin turtles can survive only in water that is not polluted. This helps scientists measure the health of wetlands.

**Massachusetts,** Garter Snake

Garter snakes hunt earthworms and amphibians. When frightened, they release an odor that may chase away **predators**.

**New York,** Snapping Turtle

Snapping turtles cannot hide their head in their shells. They have a powerful bite, or snap, that they use for protection and hunting.

**Vermont,** Painted Turtle

Painted turtles spend most of their time in the water. They can also be found resting in the sunshine on rocks.

# Unofficial State Reptiles/Amphibians

**New York,** Eastern Hellbender

At more than 2 feet (0.7 m) long, eastern hellbenders are the largest water salamanders in the United States. They live under rocks in river bottoms.

**Pennsylvania,** Eastern Massasauga Rattlesnake

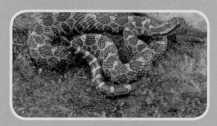

Eastern massasauga rattlesnakes have long fangs that can inject a poison called venom. They eat mice and other snakes. A "button" on the tail makes a buzzing sound when the snake is alarmed.

# Birds of the Northeast

**B**irds of all kinds live in the Northeast. Some eat plants while others eat animals. Birds are an important part of many ecosystems. Some of the region's most common birds are robins, chickadees, and bluebirds. Endangered species include a shorebird called the piping plover and the roseate tern, which is a small seabird found in New York and several New England states.

### New Hampshire, Purple Finch
Purple finches sing their own song. They also add the songs of other birds, such as the American goldfinch and the barn swallow, to their music.

### New Jersey, American Goldfinch
The American goldfinch eats only seeds. In the winter, the male's bright feathers fade, turning the same paler color as the female's.

Ruffed grouse beat their wings against the air to make a drumming noise that scares off other animals.

The black-capped chickadee can remember thousands of different spots to hide its food.

The oldest American robin on record was 13 years and 11 months old.

### Maryland, Baltimore Oriole
The Baltimore oriole takes about a week to build a nest. This medium-sized songbird eats ripe, dark-colored fruits.

### Pennsylvania, Ruffed Grouse
Ruffed grouse eat mostly plants. They are able to find food during cold winter months because they can digest tree buds and twigs.

### Vermont, Hermit Thrush
In the east, hermit thrushes usually build their nests on the ground. On the west side of the Rocky Mountains, they choose trees for their nests.

## Rhode Island,
### Rhode Island Red Chicken

Rhode Island red chickens, the official state bird, are an important food source for people. They provide high-quality eggs and plump meat.

## Connecticut,
### American Robin

American robins eat a variety of food. They tend to feed on earthworms in the morning and fruit later in the day.

## New York,
### Eastern Bluebird

Eastern bluebirds weave their nests out of grass and other fibers. Nests are found in the holes and cracks of tree trunks.

**Baltimore orioles sometimes eat by stabbing their beaks into fruit and slurping out the food.**

*Only half of blue hen chickens have blue feathers. The feathers of the rest are all black or white splashed with black.*

**Hermit thrushes hunt by quivering, or shaking grass with their feet, to find insects.**

## Massachusetts and Maine,
### Black-capped Chickadee

The black-capped chickadee is an omnivore. It stores its food in trees for as long as a month. The tiny bird weighs less than 1 ounce (30 grams).

## Delaware, Blue Hen Chicken

The blue hen chicken is Delaware's state bird. This flightless bird weighs about 5 pounds (2 kilograms).

# Plants of the Northeast

**T**rees, shrubs, grasses, and a variety of wildflowers provide food and habitat for animals throughout the Northeast. The region's deciduous and coniferous forests, wetlands, and many bodies of water give mammals, birds, insects, and fish places to thrive. The plants of the Northeast are also an important source of clean air. Healthy, plentiful plant life helps both animals and humans.

### Connecticut
**Mountain laurel**, an evergreen shrub with pink or white flowers, is also called spoonwood. American Indians used to make spoons from the plant's wood.

### Maine
**White pinecone and tassel** grows on the white pine tree. The tassel is the blue-green needle-like leaves.

*There are both male and female pinecones. The ones on the ground are females.*

*Lilacs belong to the same family of plants as olives.*

### Maryland
**Black-eyed Susan** is a member of the sunflower family. It grows east of the Rocky Mountains.

### Massachusetts
**American elm trees** can grow taller than 100 feet (30 m). Their trunks can measure 4 feet (1.2 m) wide.

### New Hampshire
**Purple lilacs** are hardy plants. Lilac bushes can live for hundreds of years.

**New Jersey**
**Common violets** grow up to 8 inches (20 cm) tall. The ancient Greeks used violets to make food, medicine, and wine more than 2,000 years ago.

**New York**
**Roses** grow in many colors, including white, yellow, pink, and red. The petals and hip, or seed pods, of the rose plant are full of nutrients.

**Pennsylvania**
**Eastern hemlock trees** can take 300 years to become full grown. This evergreen tree may live for more than 800 years.

The common violet is perennial. That means it lives, grows, and flowers for three or more years.

The black-eyed Susan is biennial. That means it lasts or lives for two years.

**Rhode Island**
**Red maples** grow quickly. Their wood is used for furniture, baskets, and crates.

**Delaware**
**Peach blossoms** are light pink or purple flowers. They grow on peach trees in spring, before the leaves and fruit appear.

**Vermont**
**Sugar maple trees** can live for 400 years. Their sap is used to make maple syrup.

# Challenges Facing the Northeast

**H**uman activity, such as cutting down trees for lumber or to clear land for development, is decreasing the size of Northeast forests. The region's natural areas may also be affected by **climate change**, which can produce more severe storms. In recent years, powerful hurricanes have hit many parts of the eastern United States. High winds and heavy rainfall result in fast-rising rivers and widespread flooding. These natural disasters damage ecosystems across the region.

In much of the Northeast, winter brings strong winds, bitter cold, and snowfall. However, the region's plants and animals have **adapted** to live in this climate. The maple, beech, and birch trees that are common in the Northeast, for example, have survived there for millions of years. A change to a warmer climate might threaten these forests.

# Human Impact

Humans may affect climate change in different ways. Some of the heat reaching Earth from the Sun is captured by carbon dioxide and other gases in the **atmosphere**. In the past century, many scientists believe, the amount of carbon dioxide in the atmosphere has increased as a result of human activities. These activities include burning coal, gasoline, and other products made from oil. Scientists believe this helps cause climate change. Many people think humans need to reduce their use of such fuels to avoid harmful effects of a changing climate.

🌿 In a flash flood, rushing water caused by heavy rains or melting snow overflows low-lying land in a sudden burst.

🌿 Forest management programs sometimes use arborists, or tree specialists, to help support a local ecosystem. Cutting white birches, for example, increases the sunlight for sugar maple trees.

# Northeast Forests

Some scientists believe that by the year 2100, forests of maple, birch, and beech trees could disappear from the Northeast. One result would be the loss of various plant and animal species that depend on those trees.

**A sugar maple tree usually must grow for**

**40 years** before it can be tapped for syrup.

Yellow birch bark can be used to light fires, even if it is wet.

**American beech trees are able to grow in the shade of other taller trees, such as maples.**

# Endangered
# Species Spotlight

**B**lue whales are a type of **baleen**, or toothless, whale. When the whale opens its mouth, water rushes in. Then, the water filters back out through the baleen, leaving food inside the mouth. Baleen whales have two **blowholes**. The blue whale can measure 100 feet (30 m) long and weigh 200 tons (180 tonnes). During the 20th century, more than 360,000 blue whales were hunted for oil, which was used for lamp fuel, soap, and other products. Today, only 10,000 to 25,000 blue whales live in their natural habitat.

Sperm whales are toothed whales. Toothed whales have one blowhole. Sperm whales live in the deep waters of the world's oceans. This makes it difficult to count their numbers. Scientists believe there are between 200,000 and 1.5 million sperm whales alive today. Over the past 200 years, hunters have taken as many as one million of these toothed whales. Today, whales that come to the water surface to breathe may hit ships, which can often be deadly. Pollution of water habitats is another concern.

The North Atlantic right whale is an endangered baleen species.

The shortnose sturgeon is a fish species that lives mostly in the region's rivers. These bony fish have lived in the Northeast since dinosaurs roamed the land more than 65 million years ago. Female shortnose sturgeons can live more than 65 years, but males usually do not live past 30 years. The main threats to this species are pollution and changes to its habitat. Dams and factories along northeastern rivers have caused these fish to disappear from many areas.

The shortnose sturgeon, less than 5 feet (1.5 m) long, is the smallest species of sturgeon in the Northeast.

## Get Involved

Seven out of 13 baleen whale species are endangered. Hunters continue to take more than 1,000 whales every year, even though it is against the law. Industry, noise, and water pollution force whales from their feeding grounds. The farther they have to swim to find food, the more energy they have to use. Climate change is also affecting marine habitats. When food sources die out or move to different areas, the whales must leave as well.

You can get involved in efforts to protect whales. The website of the organization Save the Whales helps educate children and adults about marine mammals and their environment. You can also find out more about how to help protect whales around the world.

For more information, visit the Save the Whales organization at www. savethewhales.org/ you_can_do.html.

# Activity

**A** plant or animal species introduced by human activity to an ecosystem can do a great deal of harm. This type of plant or animal is called an invasive species. An example of this kind of species in the Northeast is the hemlock woolly adelgid.

This tiny insect, native to Asia, was accidentally brought from southern Japan more than 50 years ago. Since then, the numbers of adelgids in the Northeast has increased greatly. The insects threaten the health of certain hemlock tree populations. When the adelgids feed on tree sap, they damage and may even introduce poison into the tree. Plants in the adelgid's new habitats are not adapted to protect themselves from this invasive species. Another problem is that the adelgid's predators do not live in these areas to help control the insect's population.

🌿 Adelgid egg sacs, or bags, look like bits of cotton attached to the underside of hemlock branches.

# Make an Ecosystem Web

Many species rely on the hemlock tree for survival. Use this book, and research on the internet, to find out what plants and animals live in a hemlock forest.

1. Create an ecosystem web of a hemlock forest. Include hemlock trees and the plants or animals that live alongside them.
2. Write down the role hemlock trees play in the lives of the other species.
3. Now, introduce the hemlock woolly adelgid to your web.
4. Remove the hemlocks from the web to show that the insects will kill the trees after a few years.
5. Write down what you think will happen to each of the other species in your web. Will they stay there, move somewhere else, or die?
6. Discuss with your classmates and family the long-term effects of hemlocks being gone from the forest.

## Sample Ecosystem Web

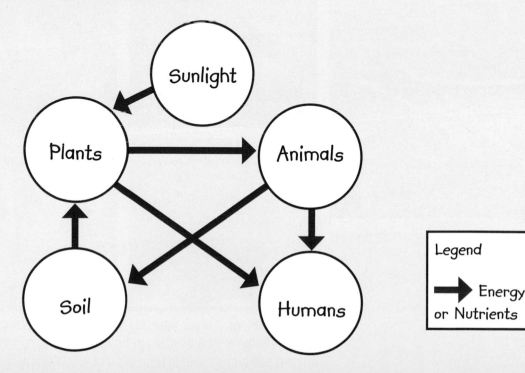

# Quiz

**1** What ocean borders the Northeast?

**2** What is an herbivore?

**3** Which two Great Lakes does the Niagara River flow between?

**4** Which major Northeast river begins at a beaver pond?

**5** Why do people call beavers "nature's engineers"?

**6** How many frog and toad species exist in the world?

**7** Where do hermit thrushes usually build their nests?

**8** To what family of flowers do black-eyed Susans belong?

**9** What are the layers of gas surrounding Earth called?

**10** How many species of baleen whales are endangered?

ANSWERS: 1. Atlantic 2. A plant-eating animal 3. Erie and Ontario 4. Connecticut 5. Because they build dams so well 6. About 3,500 7. On the ground 8. Sunflower 9. The atmosphere 10. Seven

# Key Words

**adapted:** changed to fit a specific situation

**atmosphere:** the layers of gas surrounding Earth

**baleen:** bristle-like structures that hang down from a baleen whale's upper jaw

**blowholes:** holes for breathing in the top of the head of whales and other animals

**carnivores:** animals that feed mostly on other animals

**climate change:** a change in average temperatures and other weather conditions over a long period of time, such as the warming trend that most scientists believe has been taking place over the past century

**climates:** usual weather conditions of regions over a long period of time

**cold-blooded:** having a body temperature that changes with the environment's temperature

**dams:** barriers across a waterway that control the flow of water

**deciduous:** losing leaves each winter

**endangered:** at risk of no longer surviving on Earth or in a particular region

**glaciers:** giant slabs of ice that move slowly down a slope or across land over time

**habitats:** the places where animals or plants naturally live

**larvae:** the wingless forms of newly hatched insects

**mammals:** animals that have hair or fur and drink milk from the mother

**native:** originating and growing in a certain place

**natural resources:** things found in the environment that have value as a source of food or energy or that can be used for making products

**nutrients:** substances that living things need to survive and grow

**omnivores:** animals that eat plants and animals

**plateau:** a raised area of land with a flat top

**predators:** animals that hunt other animals for food

**scales:** small, stiff plates that form the outer covering of some types of animals

**species:** a group of similar animals or plants

**tundra:** a region with a cold climate that has few plants and no trees

**wetlands:** lowland areas wholly or partly covered with water

# Index

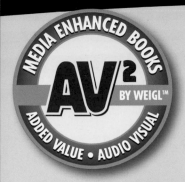

# Log on to www.av2books.com

AV² by Weigl brings you media enhanced books that support active learning. Go to www.av2books.com, and enter the special code found on page 2 of this book. You will gain access to enriched and enhanced content that supplements and complements this book. Content includes video, audio, weblinks, quizzes, a slide show, and activities.

## AV² Online Navigation

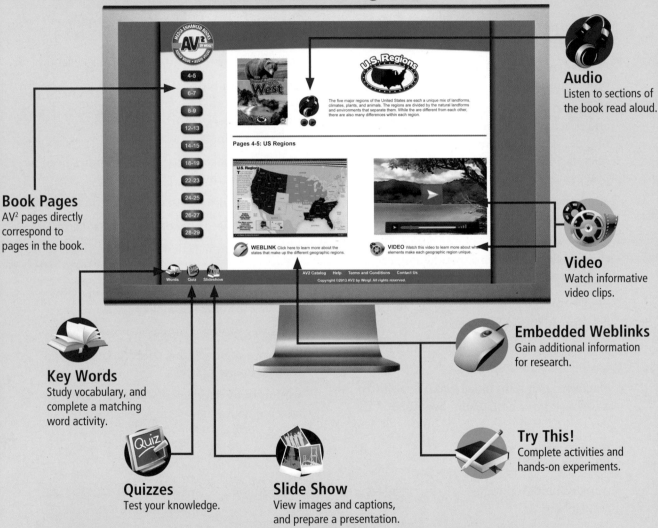

**Book Pages**
AV² pages directly correspond to pages in the book.

**Key Words**
Study vocabulary, and complete a matching word activity.

**Quizzes**
Test your knowledge.

**Slide Show**
View images and captions, and prepare a presentation.

**Audio**
Listen to sections of the book read aloud.

**Video**
Watch informative video clips.

**Embedded Weblinks**
Gain additional information for research.

**Try This!**
Complete activities and hands-on experiments.

AV² was built to bridge the gap between print and digital. We encourage you to tell us what you like and what you want to see in the future.

## Sign up to be an AV² Ambassador at www.av2books.com/ambassador.